Make no little plans; they have no magic to stir men's minds.

—Daniel H. Burnham, American architect and construction chief of the 1893 World's Fair

For my darling Daulat and in memory of his father, engineer Mantravadi Lajpat Rai. —K.G.D.

To Ann and Rachel. Thanks for all of your encouragement! —G.F.

The text of this book is set in Charter ITC.
The illustrations are digital mixed media with ink and watercolor.

Library of Congress Cataloging-in-Publication Data is on file.

ISBN: 978-0-547-95922-1

Manufactured in China | SCP 10 9 8 7 6 5 4 3 2 1 | 4500473564

MR. FERRIS AND HIS WHEEL

Written by **Kathryn Gibbs Davis**

Illustrated by **Gilbert Ford**

It was only ten months until the next World's Fair. But everyone was still talking about the star attraction of the *last* World's Fair. At eighty-one stories, France's Eiffel Tower was the world's tallest building. Its pointy iron and air tower soared so high that visitors to the top could see Paris in one breathtaking sweep.

Completed in 1889, the Eiffel Tower stood at 986 feet, surpassing America's Washington Monument to become the world's tallest man-made structure.

Now it was America's turn to impress the world at the 1893 Chicago World's Fair. But what could outshine the famous French tower? And who would build it? A nationwide contest was announced.

CHICAGO
TRIBUNE
WORLD'S FAIR
CONTEST

Before TV and the Internet, people from around the globe gathered at World's Fairs to share their different ways of life and new technologies. Tasty inventions such as hamburgers and Cracker Jack first appeared here!

FAIR JUDGES SAY "NO"

Contest drawings poured in from around the country. But most of the plans looked like the Eiffel Tower, only bigger. The fair judges said no to every last one. Was this really the best that American engineers could muster?

To an ambitious young mechanical engineer, this contest was more than a dare. It was a matter of national pride. George Washington Gale Ferris Jr. had already designed some of the country's biggest bridges, tunnels, and roads. He could never allow a French tower to overshadow America's World's Fair. Why, hadn't the United States built the world's first skyscraper? George had seen the elegant steel frame rise ten stories high with his own eyes.

Supported by a metal frame instead of solid walls, Chicago's Home Insurance building was the world's first skyscraper. Birdcages were the inspiration for the metal frame.

George had an idea, an idea for a structure that would dazzle and *move*, not just stand still like the Eiffel Tower.

Back at his drawing board in Pittsburgh, he and his engineering partner, William Gronau, measured and remeasured. A mistake of even an inch could bring their invention crashing down.

George arrived in Chicago and made his case
to the construction chief of the fair.

The chief stared at George's drawings. No one had ever
created a fair attraction that huge and complicated. The chief
told George that his structure was "so flimsy it would collapse."

George had heard enough. He rolled up his drawings and said,
"You are an architect, sir. I am an engineer."

George knew something the chief did not. His invention would
be delicate-looking *and* strong. It would be both stronger and lighter
than the Eiffel Tower because it would be built with an amazing new
metal—steel.

George was a steel expert, and his structure would be made of a steel alloy. Alloys combine a super-strong mix of a hard metal with two or more chemical elements.

The judges could not decide. Fall turned to winter as they dilly-dallied. In only four months the fair would open, and it still had no star attraction. Finally, desperate, they agreed to give George's far-fetched idea a try. But they would not give him one penny for the materials to build it.

The clock was ticking. George dashed from bank to bank, asking for help. But when he began describing his invention, lenders laughed him into the street. So George used his own savings and convinced a few wealthy investors to join him. Still short of money, he boldly went ahead and ordered the parts he needed from a dozen different steel mills.

In January 1893, George's construction crew began work on the foundation. Shovels broke as the workers tried digging into the frozen ground. It was one of the most brutally cold winters in Chicago history.

Blast! George ordered his crew to dynamite the icy earth. But what they found underneath was scarier still.

Quicksand! The deadly muck could suck man or machine under in seconds.

"The frost at the wheel site was three feet deep; the quicksand was 20 feet in depth and saturated with water," said Luther V. Rice, construction and operations manager. "Pumps were kept running night and day to keep out the water and live steam had to be used to thaw the sand and broken stone."

George and his brave workers kept frantically digging. Finally, thirty-five feet down, they hit solid ground. They planted two huge steel towers deep into the earth, bolted them to crossbars of steel, and poured in cement to hold it all in place. Then they carefully

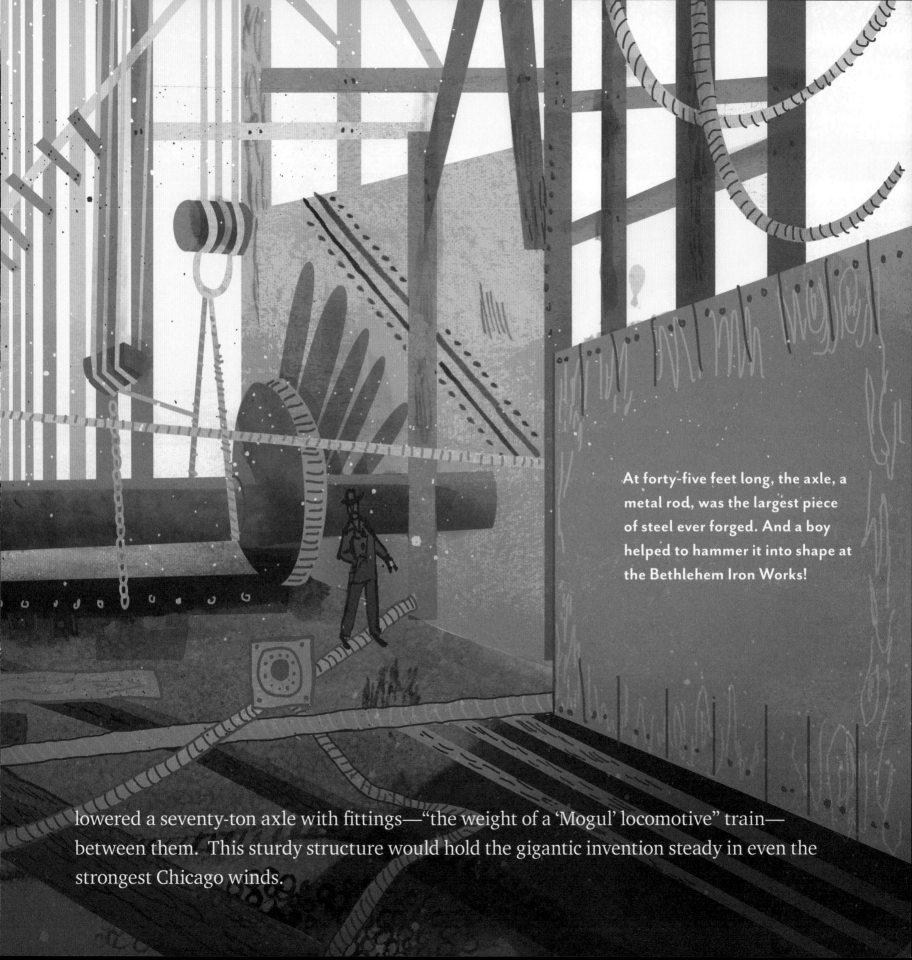

At forty-five feet long, the axle, a metal rod, was the largest piece of steel ever forged. And a boy helped to hammer it into shape at the Bethlehem Iron Works!

lowered a seventy-ton axle with fittings—"the weight of a 'Mogul' locomotive" train—between them. This sturdy structure would hold the gigantic invention steady in even the strongest Chicago winds.

As time grew shorter, freight trains from all over the country chugged onto the fairgrounds, loaded with more than 100,000 parts. Workers hurried to fit all the pieces together like a giant Lego toy. Hammers pounded nonstop in the breathless race to finish. Responsible for the wheel's many structural details, George's partner was losing hope.

"Frequently I was discouraged and ready to give up. But, through the encouragement of Mr. Ferris, work was always resumed."

—William Gronau

Finally, with only two months left, the last section was bolted into place.

And there stood a perfect, enormous circle: 834 feet in circumference, rising 265 feet above the ground, and designed to move with the precision of the smallest watch. It looked exactly how George had first imagined it back as a boy on his ranch in Nevada.

Living near the shore of Nevada's Carson River, George had often watched the water wheel turn around and around. Many times he had imagined shrinking to the size of one of his toy soldiers and hitching a ride up, up, and away in one of its wooden buckets.

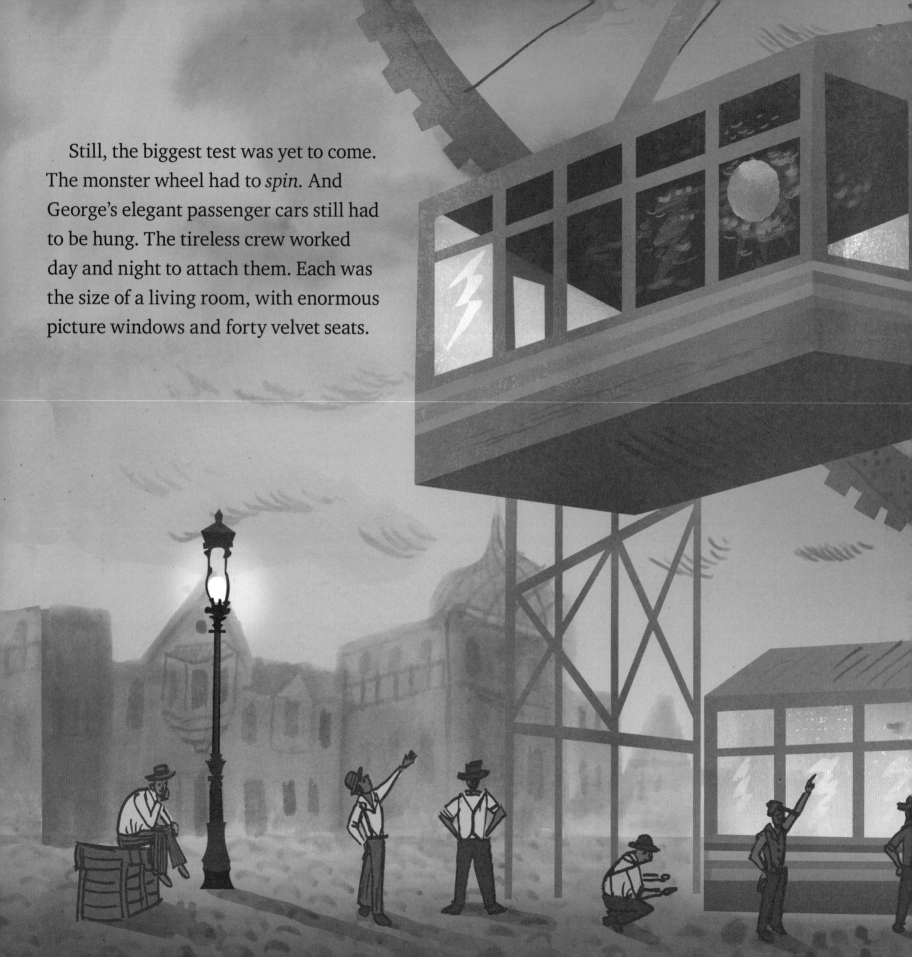

Still, the biggest test was yet to come.
The monster wheel had to *spin*. And
George's elegant passenger cars still had
to be hung. The tireless crew worked
day and night to attach them. Each was
the size of a living room, with enormous
picture windows and forty velvet seats.

George's wheel worked like a bicycle wheel. Both are supported by skinny, flexible rods called spokes. As the wheel turns, the spokes work together to share the weight. These are called tension wheels.

On June 21, 1893, opening day finally arrived. Two thousand people gathered as flags waved. George took the stage and dedicated his wheel to the noble profession of engineering. Then George's wife presented him with a beautiful golden whistle.

George and his wife stepped proudly into Car Number One, followed by their nervous but excited guests. Uniformed guards closed and locked the door. Would the wheel work?

George blew the golden whistle. Two thousand tons of steel began to turn around as the soft clanking of a large chain drove the mighty machine. Up, up, up the car quietly floated above the mud and noise.

Two steam engines (an extra one in case one broke) made the wheel turn. George had hidden them under the wooden platform where riders boarded.

As the car was lifted higher everyone rose from the velvet seats and crowded to the windows. Spread out below them was a dizzying sweep of the fairgrounds, the city of Chicago, and sparkling Lake Michigan— and even glimpses of three faraway states!

Below, more cars were loaded, and after the people had gone two times around and had twenty glorious airborne minutes in motion, powerful brakes brought the wheel to a whisper-soft stop. When the conductor called "All out!" everyone begged to go around again.

The wheel is safe! The news raced through the fairgrounds, through the city of Chicago, and across the country.

All summer, visitors from around the world traveled to the Chicago World's Fair. It didn't matter whether one was a senator, a farmer, a boy or girl. Everyone wanted to take a spin on the magnificent wheel. Adventurous couples asked to get married on it! On hot, steamy days, the wheel was the perfect place to escape up, up, up into the cooling breezes. All you needed was fifty cents.

CLOSETS
~ AND ~
WASH
ROOMS
←

During the nineteen weeks the wheel was in operation, 1.5 million passengers rode it. It revolved more than 10,000 times, withstood gale-force winds and storms, and did not need one repair.

At night, George Ferris's wheel became a magical glowing circle with 3,000 electric light bulbs—another brand-new invention.

As the Queen of the Midway made its stately rotation, so did the seasons. Soon a fall chill filled the air, and fair visitors began to thin out.

In the late 1800s, homes were still lit with candles and kerosene lamps. The Chicago World's fair helped reassure people that electricity was safe. At night, farmers and sailors from as far away as forty miles could see the wheel's spectacular blaze of lights.

On October 26, 1893, just before midnight, the immense twinkling, spinning circle slowed to its final stop. The Chicago World's Fair was over. George had called his creation a Monster Wheel, but his investors renamed it after its inventor: the Ferris Wheel.

The Chicago Fair, or the "White City," inspired two more magical places—the Emerald City in the classic children's book *The Wonderful Wizard of Oz* by L. Frank Baum, and Disneyland. Walt Disney's father was a construction worker on the fair. He told his son stories about the dreamlike city he had helped build, and young Walt grew up to build famous amusement parks that stay open all year round.

Visitors returned to their homes to tell the story of the world's greatest ride, and before long copies of the Ferris Wheel began popping up around the world. In 1894, the next Ferris wheel appeared in California on a cliff overlooking the Pacific Ocean. Lit up at night, it was the first landmark seen by ships finding their way home.

Today, Ferris wheels are the most familiar and beloved carnival ride at state fairs and amusement parks. A ride on one still feels like flying to the moon— and oh-oh-oooh, the view!

Since 1893, there have been over eight tallest-ever Ferris wheels. And the race continues. The current record holder for the world's tallest is the Singapore Flyer at 541 feet.

QUOTE SOURCES

"so flimsy it would collapse": *The Ferris Wheel*, centennial edition, compiled by Lois Stodieck Jones for the Carson Valley Historical Society. The Grace Dangberg Foundation, 1993.

"You are an architect, sir": Ibid.

"Was three feet deep": Luther V. Rice, "Ferris Wheel." Report of the Committee on Awards of the World's Columbian Commission. Government Printing Office, 1901.

"the weight of a 'Mogul'": Carl Snyder, "Engineer Ferris and His Wheel." *Review of Reviews: An International Magazine* (American edition) 8, September 1893.

And a boy helped: Ibid.

"Frequently I was discouraged": "The Great Wheel at Chicago." *Scientific American,* July 1, 1893.

"I determined that . . .": "He built the Great Wheel—Engineer Ferris Tells Why and How He Did It." *The Atchinson Daily Globe,* Atchinson, Kansas, August 29, 1893.

SELECTED BIBLIOGRAPHY

Anderson, Norman D. *Ferris Wheels: An Illustrated History.* 1993.

Anderson, Norman D., and Walter Brown. *Ferris Wheels.* Pantheon, 1983.

Applebaum, Stanley. *The Chicago's World Fair of 1893: A Photographic Record.* Dover Architectural Series, Dover Publications, June 1, 1980.

Bombs and Bones: A Ferris Family Tree. www.ferristree.com.

Larson, Erik. *Devil in the White City: Murder, Magic and Madness at the Fair That Changed America.* Vintage, 2003.

Lawson, Robert. *The Great Wheel.* Walker, 1993. First published 1957 by Viking.

Klasey, Jack. "Who Invented the Ferris Wheel?" *American History Illustrated* (Sept/Oct. 1993): 60–63.

Meehan, Patrick. "The Big Wheel." Hyde Park Historical Society, spring 2000 newsletter.

Obituary of George W. G. Ferris "Inventor Ferris Is Dead." *New York Times,* November 23, 1896.

Weingardt, Richard G. *Circles in the Sky: The Life and Times of George Ferris.* American Society of Civil Engineers, 2009.

WEBSITES

Chicago's Hyde Park Historical Society Page: *The Big Wheel.* www.hydeparkhistory.org/kids/wheel.html.

The History of Theme Park Inventions: *The Ferris Wheel.* www.inventors.about.com/od/+startinventions/ss/theme_park.htm.

Internet Fairground History: Ferris Wheel Research. library.thinkquestion.org/C002926/history/ferris1.html.

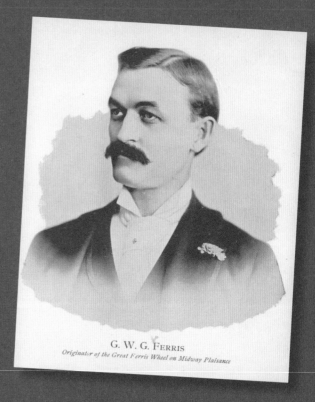

G. W. G. FERRIS
Originator of the Great Ferris Wheel on Midway Plaisance

Official photograph of George Washington Gale Ferris Jr., taken from the Chicago World's Fair pamphlet. Ferris was thirty-four years old.

Photograph courtesy of Douglas County Historical Society.